OUTSIDE NOW

March and April

Trevor Terry and
Margaret Linton

Bell & Hyman

Contents

The Weatherman

I wonder if you keep a weather chart in your classroom? If you do, it is sometimes fun to ask yourself questions. In March and in April you could ask questions like these.

1. How many different kinds of weather have we had?
2. How many days have been windy?
3. How many days have been sunny?
4. Have there been more rainy days than dry days?

Perhaps you can think of some other questions.

We often have wind, sunshine and showers at this time of the year. We talk about 'March winds' and 'April showers'. What do you draw on the weather chart to show a windy day? Here are some ideas.

Kites flying　　　Washing flapping　　　Trees bending

Wind comes from different directions. An arrow on a weather map tells us from which direction the wind is coming. A number tells us how fast the wind is travelling. Look at the map on the next page.

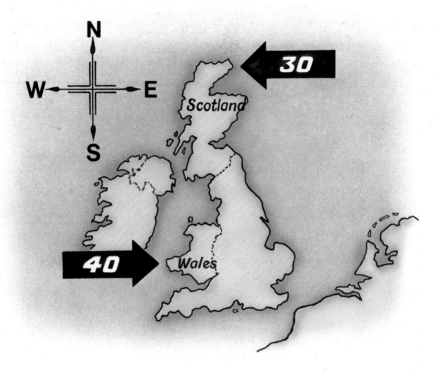

In Wales the wind is coming from the West. It is travelling at 40 miles per hour. When wind travels at about 40 miles per hour, we call it a gale. Sometimes the wind travels faster than this. Strong gales can do a lot of damage.

When wind moves slowly, we call it a breeze. We talk about strong winds and gentle breezes.

Look at the map again. Which way is the wind coming from in Scotland?

March and April are full of surprises. The weather can change very suddenly. One day it feels quite warm. The next day might be cold. Sometimes it even snows. Then it seems more like Winter.

Perhaps for one week you could make a very big weather chart like this one. Divide the section for each day into two. Draw two weather pictures each day, one in the morning and one in the afternoon. Count how many times the weather changes in one week.

Springtime

March and April are exciting months. There is so much to see. Animals and plants are waking up after their Winter sleep. Everywhere around us things are happening.

Here are seven things to look out for. They all show us that Spring is here.

1. If you go into the country you may see new born lambs. They are full of life and grow quickly. In about two weeks, lambs weigh twice as much as they did when they were born.

New born lamb

2. Rooks build their nests in tall trees. A group of their nests is called a rookery. Each nest is between 40 and 50 centimetres across. Rooks build them with twigs, and line them with leaves and grass. Sometimes they steal from other nests.

Rookery

At the end of March they lay three to five greenish eggs marked with brown blotches. The eggs hatch in about 18 days. The parents feed the chicks on worms and grubs. The chicks grow quickly. By the end of May they are ready to fly away.

3. Buds are beginning to swell and burst open. Have you noticed that buds on some kinds of trees open into leaves before the buds on other trees?

Buds opening

4. Do you remember seeing daffodil bulbs in the Autumn? Perhaps you planted some. Most daffodil bulbs flower in April.

Daffodils

After the flowers have faded, the leaves make more food. The food is stored in the bulbs. It will help to make more daffodil flowers next Spring.

5. You find conkers under horse chestnut trees. They drop from the trees in the Autumn. In Spring each conker puts out a strong root. We say that the conker is germinating. Conkers are the seeds of the horse chestnut tree. When seeds grow, they germinate.

Germinating conkers

9

6. Crocuses can be mauve or yellow or white. These crocuses flower in the park every Spring at the beginning of March.

Crocuses

7. The swallows which flew away to Africa last Autumn, come back in the middle of April. House martins come back too. You can tell the swallows by their long forked tails.

Will you be the first to see the swallows this year?

Swallows

You may not be able to see all these things, but perhaps you will see other signs of Spring.

Places to nest

Everyone likes birds. We like to see them in our streets and gardens. We enjoy listening to their singing. As the days get longer, the birds sing more. They begin to build their nests too. At nesting time, birds need quietness. They need to be left alone.

Here is a mistle thrush caring for its babies. Birds of the same kind usually choose the same sort of nesting place. Mistle thrushes build their nests in trees.

Mistle thrush

Birds have a special way of knowing, which we call instinct. They don't think about building, as we would, but they know where to build their nests. We say that they know by instinct.

All kinds of things are used in nest building. Here are some of them.

twigs   grasses   roots   feathers
moss   mud   string   paper

Birds choose some of these things for building their nests. They don't think about it. They choose by instinct.

This heron knows by instinct that the right place to build is at the top of a tall tree.

Heron

Linnet

In the same way, this linnet knows that the right place to nest is in a bush. It has chosen a bramble bush.

Swans always build their nests on the ground. They choose somewhere close to a river or a lake. When the young swans, called cygnets, hatch out, they are able to swim on the water nearby.

Swan

Some birds use holes for their nests. This tawny owl has chosen a hole in an old birch tree. ▼

Song thrush ▲

Tawny owl

Sometimes birds choose rather odd places to build in. We don't know why this is. This song thrush has chosen to build its nest in some old rusty machinery.

Places to grow

Plants need soil, water and sunlight to grow. Some plants seem to grow almost anywhere. Others grow better in their own special places.

Here are some places where you can see wild flowers in March and April.

Lawns. You will often see daisies growing on lawns where the grass is short. Daisies grow close to the ground and need plenty of sunlight.

Daisies

Dandelions

The roadside. Grass by the roadside is longer. Some plants grow well in longer grass. Dandelions seem to grow in most places, but we see lots of them flowering by the roadside.

Shady places. Some plants grow better where there is shade. These celandines are growing where it is shady and damp. Celandines are often found near streams. Their flowers close up at night. Daisy and dandelion flowers close up at night too.

Celandines

Primroses

Banks and ditches. Where the soil is good, primroses often grow on banks and on the sides of ditches. They grow in woods too. These beautiful flowers should not be picked.

Heaths. Soil on heaths is dry and sandy. Most plants need better soil, but gorse bushes grow well on heaths. In the Spring, heaths are often covered with golden gorse.

Gorse

15

Looking at buds

Have you ever looked closely at a tree bud? Perhaps there are some on your Nature Table. Look at them again. They are not all the same, are they? Each kind of tree has its own special buds.

Inside the buds are new leaves. The leaves are folded together very tightly. The picture shows you a sycamore bud cut in half. Can you see all the leaves folded together?

Sycamore bud cut in half

The outside parts of a bud are called scales. They protect the leaves inside. As the weather gets warmer, the leaves grow bigger. They push the scales open. The new leaves burst out.

A sycamore bud. Can you see the bud scales?

Leaves pushing the scales open

New leaves

Look at some buds for a few days. Watch them open. You could draw the buds to show how they change. Put the date on each drawing.

Little Brook Farm

It was a lovely April morning. The farmer's wife walked across the farmyard to the small barn. She was going to see if the new lambs were alright. Over in the corner, Black Jack was lying on some sacks. He was fast asleep in the sunshine.

Inside the barn, the new lambs were with their mothers. They were in pens made from bales of straw. In one pen there were twin lambs. In the next pen another new lamb was feeding from its mother. The three lambs had been born the night before. The farmer's wife had got up in the night to help the two ewes to have their lambs.

Back in the farmhouse, the farmer was finishing his work in the office. He had to keep notes about things bought and sold. Bills had to be paid. Forms had to be filled in. He was always glad when the office work was finished.

He put down his pen. "I must go up to Primrose Hill" he said to himself. "Jim should have finished sowing the turnips by now. I want him to start planting the potatoes in High Field. The weather is just right, but we might get some rain in a day or two."

At the back door the farmer met his wife. "Come round to the back of the barn" she said. "I've something to show you." Behind the barn they saw a hen with some fluffy chicks. They were running all around her. Some were trying to get under her to keep warm. "The eggs in the nest under the bushes must have hatched this morning" said the farmer's wife.

The farmer and his wife walked back across the farmyard. "Where's Black Jack?" asked the farmer. "He was asleep over there just now" said his wife. "He must have gone off by himself." "I'll have to go without him, then" said the farmer.

Black Jack had gone up to the Old Mill.
Long ago it had ground the corn on the farm.
He got in through a hole at the bottom of the
door. Inside it was dark and dusty. He sniffed
some old sacks. Sometimes there were rats and
mice about. He liked exploring the Mill.

When he came out, some
jackdaws were flying
around. They were
nesting in holes at
the top of the Mill.
Black Jack had
scared them.

Black Jack ran over to Holly Wood. He was
not supposed to go there. The pheasants would
soon be nesting. The farmer would be cross if
he scared them.

He ran into the wood. A pheasant saw him.
It made a loud shrill call. It flew up into the
trees. A flock of pigeons in the trees flew out.
Their flapping wings made a lot of noise.
Black Jack ran out of the wood and stopped.
He looked up. There was the farmer looking at
him. Black Jack lay down. He knew he had
done wrong.

"You are a bad dog" said the farmer.
Black Jack stood up. He put his nose into the
farmer's hand. The farmer laughed. "That's to
tell me you're sorry, is it?" he said. "Alright,
you can come with me to High Field. We'll see
how Jim is getting on with the potato
planting."

Living in water

Spring is a good time to look at ponds and streams. All kinds of plants and creatures live in them and near them. Always be careful when you explore places near water.

Pond ▲   Stream ▶

Water in ponds and streams is now a little warmer. Plants are beginning to grow again. Frogs, newts and many small creatures are starting to breed.

Water birds like these mallard ducks are nesting on the banks.

Mallard ducks

You will see that some plants live close to water. We call them marsh plants. This plant is called a marsh marigold.

▼

Marsh marigolds

Frogbit and tiny duckweed

Some plants grow on top of the water. They have floating leaves. Their roots hang in the water.

Plants like Canadian pondweed live under the water. In sunlight they make oxygen. Fish and other creatures breathe the oxygen in the water. They must have oxygen to live.

This fish uses oxygen

◀ Canadian pondweed makes oxygen

We can't easily see what is happening under water. If you have an aquarium, you can look into the water. An aquarium is like a tiny pond. You can learn a lot about pond creatures if you have an aquarium.

Aquarium

Jam jars are useful for looking at things closely.

Frog spawn

Tadpoles hatching ten days later

When these tadpoles hatched, they were put into an aquarium. Later on, the baby frogs were taken back to the pond where the spawn was found.

Here are some other creatures you can learn about.

Pond snails. They lay their eggs on water plants. The eggs change into tiny snails.

Pond snail

Water beetles. There are many different kinds of water beetles. Watch them using their legs to swim through the water. See how they come to the top of the water to breathe air.

The great diving beetle feeds on other small creatures. It should be kept in its own aquarium and fed on tiny pieces of raw meat.

▼

Great diving beetle

Caddis fly larva   ▲

Caddis fly larvae. These are the young of the caddis fly. They live in cases made of pieces of plants. Sometimes they use grains of sand. Watch them pulling their homes behind them. They can breathe under water like fish.

Ponds and streams are special places. We need to take care of them.

Teachers' Notes

Since early Spring weather is so variable, weather recording can create a greater interest than usual. This might be a good time to observe some of the changes in the weather, and to record them in chart form. Tradition has it that March is a windy month, so it could be appropriate to carry out some simple investigations into this aspect of the weather.

Investigations and Activities

Wind direction

- Look at available evidence from cloud movement, smoke, pieces of paper being blown along etc.
- Hold up (a) a wet finger (b) a handkerchief.
- Look at weather vanes in the neighbourhood and in books. Note interesting designs.
- Make and use a simple weather vane.
- Make and use a wind sock.
- Study and use a magnetic compass. Consider cardinal points, and relate them to the school site.

Wind strength

- Walk into the wind holding a large sheet of thick cardboard.
- Make and use simple wind force meters. Reference books describe several easily made types.
- Investigate wind strength at different places around the school, using a ventimeter.
- Investigate wind strength at similar distances from each side of a tall wall or hedge.

Displays

- Make a picture display showing various uses of wind power, e.g. windpumps, wind driven electricity generators, sailing craft and historic windmills. The destructive force of the wind can be shown by including pictures of gale damage.
- Encourage children to record their observations of changeable Spring weather on weather charts.

Some ideas for topic work, relating to these months, are shown in the flow diagrams.

Signs of spring

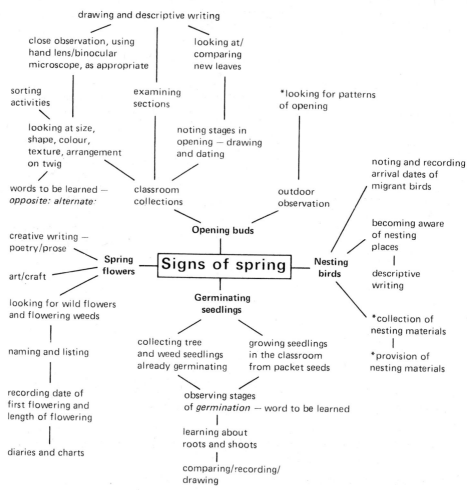

*NOTES

Patterns of opening: e.g. Do all the buds on a tree open at the same time? Do buds on the same kinds of trees open at the same time? Which buds open first/last? Does it make any difference where the tree is growing? etc.

Nesting materials: Make a collection of twigs, grasses, roots, feathers, moss, string and paper. Fill net bags with a range of these materials and hang the bags on a branch or a bird table. Encourage the children to observe, discuss and record bird activity.

Places to live

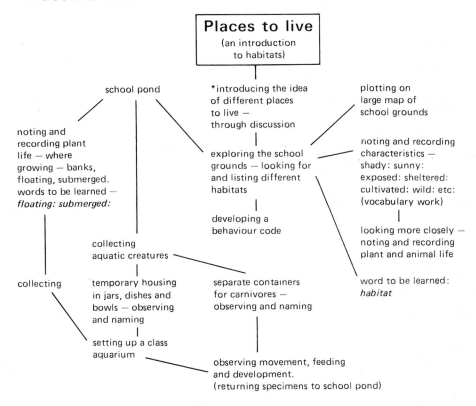

Places to live
(an introduction to habitats)

*introducing the idea of different places to live — through discussion

exploring the school grounds — looking for and listing different habitats

developing a behaviour code

school pond

noting and recording plant life — where growing — banks, floating, submerged. words to be learned — *floating: submerged:*

collecting aquatic creatures

collecting

temporary housing in jars, dishes and bowls — observing and naming

setting up a class aquarium

separate containers for carnivores — observing and naming

observing movement, feeding and development. (returning specimens to school pond)

plotting on large map of school grounds

noting and recording characteristics — shady: sunny: exposed: sheltered: cultivated: wild: etc: (vocabulary work)

looking more closely — noting and recording plant and animal life

word to be learned: *habitat*

*NOTES

Work on habitats can continue throughout most of the school year. It is helpful if an initial survey of the school grounds can be carried out by the teacher. Some of the following habitats will be found in most grounds.

under stones and decaying logs	mown grassland
trees and undergrowth	waste ground
holes and crevices	flower beds
surface of a wall	tree stumps
paths and paving	school pond

Groups of children can be encouraged to 'adopt' one or more habitats, observing and recording over a period of time. They can be helped to develop their own behaviour code, learning to walk carefully, to collect with due regard to conservation, to replace logs and stones after searching and so on.

Bibliography

A Field Guide to the Birds of Britain and Europe. Peterson R., Mountford G. and Hollom P. A. D., Collins

Fresh Water Life of the British Isles. Clegg J., Warne

Weathercraft. Smith L. P., Blandford

Nature Study and Science. Finch I., Longman

Teaching Science to Infants. Showell R., Ward Lock Educational

Trees, Stages 1 and 2 (Science 5/13). Schools Council, Macdonald Educational

Early Experiences (Sciences 5/13). Schools Council, Macdonald Educational

Using the Environment: 2. Investigations Part 2 (Science 5/13). Schools Council, Macdonald Educational

Acknowledgements

The publishers would like to thank the following for supplying the photographs on the pages indicated:
Heather Angel; 26 (TR), 28 (R).
Bruce Coleman; 28 (L).
Reg Jones; 11, 12 (both), 13 (all).
Trevor Terry; all other photographs.

First published 1985 by Bell & Hyman Limited
Denmark House, 37–39 Queen Elizabeth Street, London SE1 2QB
© Linton and Terry 1985

Terry, T.   ISBN 0 7135 2412 X
    Outside Now : March/April.
    1. Months
    I. Title   II. Linton, Margaret, 1927–
    529'.2   CE85

Phototypeset by Tradespools, Frome, Somerset
Colour Separation by Positive Colour Limited, Essex
Printed and bound in Great Britain by Purnell & Sons Limited